NORTH OF ALL BORDERS

Poems 1996-2018

Irene Hossack

STUPOR MUNDI

First published 2018 by
STUPOR MUNDI – WONDER OF THE WORLD
Fife, Scotland KY14 6JF

www.stupormundibooks.wordpress.com
mundibooks@gmail.com

Designed by Stupor Mundi and set
in Garamond 11 pt.

Stupor Mundi was the name often given to the Holy Roman Emperor Frederick II of Hohenstaufen (d.1250). A man of great talents and learning, he was a lawgiver, patron of the arts and sciences, linguist and warrior whose Sixth Crusade retook Jerusalem by negotiation rather than bloodshed. His court at Palermo was described by Dante as 'the birthplace of Italian poetry.'

For my family

Irene Hossack is from Glasgow and teaches Creative Writing and Applied Linguistics at The Open University. She studied at Monash University, Melbourne, writing her doctoral dissertation on the poetry and poetics of Geoffrey Hill, and her Masters on the poetry of Charles Simic. Her poetry has been published internationally over the years.

Thanks are due to the editors of the following anthologies, journals and magazines where some of these poems first appeared: *Envoi, Aiblins, Whaur Extremes Meet, Double Bill, Gutter, Long Poem Magazine, Causeway/Cabhsair, Poetry Scotland, Poetry Nottingham International, Orbis, Iota, Skald, Links, Noman, Writing Women, New Hope International Poetry Forum, Cimarron Review, Poetry Wales*.

My grateful thanks go to Jo Falla for his patient and inspiring guidance, making this process both enjoyable and instructive. Thanks also to members of St Mungo's Mirrorball for their support, particularly my fellow Clydebuilt 3 mentees. Thanks to my writing friends of Fantoosh, Fiona, Alison, Ginny and Lin, for all the feedback, fun and friendship over the years. To my daughters Jenny and Katie for their love and encouragement, and last but not least, thank you to Paul for his enduring love and support.

Contents

Duvet Day

Take a cold wintery morning in January when the snow
is three weeks old, lying brown at the edges. Give it
the merest hint of flushed pink as light to see by, with
    a trace
of rain hiding in the low-lying clouds.
Under a king-sized eiderdown,
upon a bed as soft as cotton-wool, still warm
from last night's pleasures, decide
the day can get by without you.

Shibboleth

Glasgow's splendour is cloaked
in the remnants of her industrial age;
a yellow pea-souper rising as
her people criss-cross the ancient
cores of Kelvin, Clyde and Molendinar.
The indefinite road ahead, the lurking
invisible threats
faced with stoic
solidarity.

Being here is to be
in the condition of shadows
and bound by complex
boundaries where close-to
intimacy, transparency
and undeclared equality
are discerned by the glottal
stop and distinct
intonations
of voice.

Homesickness

On cool autumn days in Melbourne
I can smell Glasgow. Transposed,
I think it is spring
and look for lambs – lambs that aren't
far from the city, in fields
on farms like handkerchiefs,
in contrast with the spare, sprawling bush.
I imagine the almost edible aroma
of rain as it falls on untended pavements,
mingling centuries of my ancestors' dust.
When the sounds of cicadas echo in the evening,
they bring with them a quandary:
leaving me in darkness, the sun
descends to give you morning light,
migration of moon shadows
and time's disruption, this now
is your tomorrow, the past, already here.

First Memory

Looking down on my bowl of Campbell's lentil soup,
I am struck with a thought, the thought that cannot
be properly thought, yet it is my first:
I am seven years old, seated at the family dinner table,
I am here, and I don't know how I came to be,
or what it is that consists in being this child,
this me, staring at a bowl of lentil soup.

It is the origin of things which hold the answer:
liquefied vegetables, once singularly growing in soil,
grown from seed sown by a farmer
in the countryside far from here.
Unable to go beyond the seed, to know it
before, I begin again with the bowl.
Bought from a local department store, bought from
a potter, who created and painted and made it from clay,
moulded from beginnings as earth and water
in an artist's hands. I am stuck at the clay and the paint
and the potter's mind, thinking about how
we came to be here, thinking with the limitations I have,
thinking towards the impossibility
of ever getting beyond the thought that is myself.

Mellifluous

A sonnet in honour of banned words in poetry

The ineffable shard of alabaster glimmers
like gossamer in the fronds of maram grass
betwixt the host of daffodils,
shimmering in the stippled mist.
A myriad of herons flock
to the searing, balmy shores
where the whispering wind
unsheathes her surreal woes.
The abyss of eternity hides within
an intoxicating palimpsest,
shrouds the halcyon soul
lurking beneath a glittering epiphany:
here fain I vow to slay the demons
lingering in your poetic sepia loins.

Love Letter To My Family

I remember everything. I remember for instance
a birthday meal at our favourite restaurant,
all of us dancing in the hallway at the bells,
spinning on the carnival rides at the Kelvin Hall,
building snowmen in the grounds of that
awful hotel on Christmas Eve, our wildness
not welcomed there. Joints and tarot readings
late at night, Wayne's World on the TV,
eating noodles and pizza from down the road,
past the church and the City Bakeries. James Taylor,
and Shelleyan Orphan on CD.

I remember the beauty configured in snow-weighted trees
seen from the train as I travelled North, writing letters to
    absent friends,
wishing to stay here, not capturing but remaining somehow
    like this.
Lying under stars in the snow, enchanted, not feeling cold
and the dark-white-frost night lit by the moon and the
    stars.

And later, spending hours arguing lovingly
on the subject of truth and cultural difference,
trying to understand chaos theory
in between the sups from cups of Cadbury's Cream.
Resting on Sunday afternoons with the fire blazing,
hearing ghost stories from uncles with not long to go,

giving us goosebumps on our skins, making
them so vulnerable and human as if for the first
time. We all share this desire for the inexplicable,
we share a family tree in whose roots we are entwined.
Always remember,
my spirit lives amongst your chaotic laundry
and microwaved Marks and Spencer's food.

The Asylum Seekers

They must've thought,
This is it,
we can get jobs,
have a roof over our heads,
eat.

The hard bit,
they must've thought,
was getting here.
Hiding in trucks,
knuckle to knuckle,
fighting for air,
crawling through mud
in darkness,

seeking leave to remain
in London,
at least somewhere
south of The North.

After their dispersal,
getting off the bus at the Red Road flats,
must've been like crossing
another border.

The hard bit,
they must've thought,

is climbing
the thirty flights of stairs,
after walking a mile through Springburn,
to the only shop
that will take their vouchers,
but won't give them change.

Reaching the top,
under a thick grey Glasgow sky,
it's hard to know what they must've thought
when they decided to jump
and no longer seek
leave to remain.

Cherry Blossom

When Spring snows cherry blossom on the lawns
I remember Mrs Ellis – we hated each other.
Charged with my care she would watch every morning
as I begged with my parents not to leave me there,
in the stony prison of her kitchen.

I might have howled like Ginsberg
or conspired with confessional Plath,
embraced resignation with Beckett about
the interminable nows of our lives hitting like trucks
through the heart, the end of love, longings, longevity.

Witnessing the surprise of a death
in a hospital bathroom at two a.m.,
and the failed resuscitation on my bed,
I look out on Glasgow's Necropolis,
the moon catches the light
on blown cherry blossom from surrounding trees
and I decide to slay my dragons,
to follow my bliss.

My father's mother

Minnie was as strange to me as her name.
A small old lady, black hair pulled back in a tight bun
who gave me a jewel box with a ballerina inside,
dancing to the tune of 'Music Box Dancer'.

My father watched me take it from her
as we sat in her small, brown, Glasgow tenement.
Her gentle little hands, which once saved him
from drowning in the burn, showed me the key

to making the ballerina dance. I recognised
her gypsy eyes, they belonged to you and me,
our shared inheritance rarely mentioned
but through whispered stories in your absence.

Your silhouette brooded at the window,
no interest in this woman who,
I learned later, preferred nights
at the dancing over caring for you.

Her desertion formed you and me,
your lingering suspicion of the cruelty of women
precludes trust, with only the small trace of her
presence in the dance of the music box ballerina.

Closure

When I'm gone, mourn the end of sharing books and music,
lying in the scent of new-cut grass and some sunsets
we will miss, mourn the days we languished in bed, not
those
spent crying over everything. When I'm gone don't move
the furniture right away, leave it awhile before
you remove my familiarity. Don't buy new
crockery or curtains or paintings I won't recognise
hanging on our walls. Keep to your side of the bed.
When I'm gone don't be too happy when the moon still
shines
and my stars are still in the sky, leave that space for my
toothbrush and my sensuous aroma-therapy oils.
You will have a full life, find someone new too soon,
too late, I face the consequences of my weakness,
needing unqualified approval no matter what,
in the face of a life too complicated to live.

Cumbernauld (New Town)

Arria reaches out to you,
her steel arms raised as if in praise of you,
poor fading monument to concrete.
Perhaps she admires you doing it the hard way,
perhaps she's begging for your people to stay.

Turning their backs on communities of squalor,
Glaswegians spilled gladly to your hope of the new,
dreaming of lives in your town for tomorrow,
a house with a garden, and its own front door.
As kids they would play in the middens,
peever, kick the can, or heiders up the close.
We were indulged with pristine playgrounds
of witches' hats, roundabouts and swings.

But we discovered the other face of you,
the one beyond order, underpass and ramp,
with their gaudy psychaedelic flowers
and abstract Modern art.
We found our place down the Glen,
in the remnants of the Caledonian forest,
wading waist high through your jungle of ferns,
treading your carpets of bluebells,
among hornets' nests, midges and frogs.
We'd make for the gorge and the long stretch
of pipe that towered over the trickling burn,
crawl up to its slimy, curving edge

and walk within an inch of our lives.
We'd swing from frayed ropes tied to branches,
boldly reach for the other side, hoping
for freedom from the Lego fantasy
made by your planners' utopian dreams.

Never mind the ridicule of Carbuncles;
a likeness of Janus should be
carved on all your walls.

Fairy Liquid

It was the lifestyle that I craved:
my six year old self imagined
my own mother discussing the virtues
of soft, smooth hands and mild
long-lasting bubbles, with me
asking inane questions and Mummy
replying with such graceful understanding.
Strong marketing and a soothing, hypnotic tune
had me longing for this kind of mother,
or at least one who bothered to wash up.

Henry

12th August 2009

It is all *this time last week*;
getting along absently
with the everyday,
humdrum, then
an orbit shift.

It is all *how can this be
so* and a longing for
before this time
last week, when
the living were all
accounted for.

It is all another beginning,
thrust upon us in the stark
reality of this time last week.

The Night I Turned Forty

The night I turned forty I lit a lavender
scented candle to the full moon in a cloudless sky,
said goodbye to my neglectful lover
with some regret, read my brother's tarot over the phone
and took a long, lingering wish for life
to be like this for eternity. I shared a cigarette
with Katie as we talked from our hearts;
almost sixteen and all of this ahead of her.
I popped a cork on a bottle of Australian
champagne I could ill afford,
let the bubbles sparkle up my nose
and meditated on being alone, only to find
that it was not so. Venus, my ruler, was there
guarding the moon and I imagined I was,
for the first time since birth, a small part
of the universe and it felt right. I stood alone
naked to the October wind, my bedroom window
open wide to let the moonshine in and I decided
that this could possibly be what they mean
when they say, life begins.

Our Times

Monday nights you drove me to dancing class
and we would chant the rhythms of the *Ragged
Rascal Running Round the Rugged Rock*.
I made inscrutable covenants with you;
dancing to the tunes you whistled for me,
listening as you would list my honours,
naming them one by one in a nightly
ritual, with each unique recital
punctuating my goodnight kisses.
We would stay up late to watch boring
shows like International Horse Jumping
although we never knew why. When I was six
you took me to see the white horses at Largs,
though they were not horses at all. You helped
me tie my shoes and taught me how to tell
the time by the hands of a broken clock.

And now, I regret that game of squash we never had,
and the times I wished you'd gone to bed instead
of waiting up. Your invincible heart has become a lie,
unlike the broken clock upon whose face
you taught me the intricate workings
of time's past and time's to.

April

I confess
that in losing you
I lost my faith.
It's gone
as you are -
before being
alive
in my arms,
loved.
You were
to be
the completion
of our brood.
Your name
on our Christmas cards
a full stop.

Blending Families

You have learned
to cook authentic Italian tomato sauce from scratch
and save it in a jar, in another woman's kitchen.

I have learned
to leave the rainbow colours and ceiling stars
that lit your bedroom sky,
fold away your five thousand Barbie clothes
and be grown up about things.

We have lost those innocent times
when life seemed less complicated,
a playground we explored,
singing songs about nonsensical girls
like black-eyed Suzie.

When they take you for family portraits
and give you gifts in which
I no longer have a say,
I try
not to mind
that you like them.

Delivery

After all we've been through
in eight months, three weeks and thirteen hours,
the wall clock charts another beginning,
time truthfully recorded for posterity
in the nurse's log,
a time which proclaims an emptiness,
fulfilment beyond loss and absence,
the cleft and union of us.

I am fixed by your stare from the perspex cot,
your first resting place on earth beyond us,
and now you must remain exposed,
yet in the faithful trust your gaze conveys,
your birth delivers me.

You and I

We created something wonderful,
beyond what could be in our control,
whether or not we remained in love.

We received the product of our making,
and found ourselves with two miracles.
Through bath times, ear aches, school concerts,
nerves the night before exams,
we shared phrases as we kissed them goodbye:
Be the best that you can be,
keep a good heart,
don't let words hurt,
you are beautiful.

This cannot be erased,
as we have been.
Our children are living testaments
of the dreams we made together
enduring, despite our failure
to see it through.

North of All Borders

1.

I thought there would be more,
some bustle and scurry,
a doctor rushing in,
cars screaming, as I was,
to a halt outside your gate.
I thought there would be less
anguish to face as you
waited for the right time;
knowing there is a moment
before, and all afterwards.
I thought I was awake when
I was dreaming. Forgetting
to remember you had gone,
somewhere North of all borders,
with no maps for me to trace.

2.

Your leather handbag sits
impotent, with zipped compartments
I steel myself to look through;
no lipstick, no powder nor
mirror. A brown purse I don't recognise,
notes with sayings,
a birthday book with dates

written in your hand,
a pen with your initials.
I don't know what to do
with this bag resting by your bed,
you can't take it with you,
what you always said and I
never knew.

3.
We lit your final hours
with psychedelic lava lamps
and put *Search for the Hero
Inside Yourself* on repeat.
We've said goodbye so many times,
now, unutterable, hanging
silently between me, your body,
and you willing the words which I refuse.
For you, the stark rain falls
bleakness crowds our loss, while
one man of faith conducts your soul
through its final earthly hours.

4.
We remembered my birthdays
until this, when you don't sing
down the phone, out of tune.
I imagine you revelling
in your heaven, where you can

hear everything and see complete,
always dining formally
with *Pavalova* for dessert,
the silverware suitably placed.
You sleep in a four-poster bed,
surrounded by your books,
a brain surgeon in your spare time,
while I must make friends
with the necessity of dying.

5.
Having become a stranger to myself,
I clamber for the good seats,
to see what happens next. Your eyes
won't pierce me with their critical love,
your ears won't hear when you listen
for whisperings of things I get wrong.
No more bitterness for what you see
me having and wish was yours,
and yet, now knowing,
my life held no importance
to anyone but you.

6.
The beginning of Winter rain
clings to the sodden grass,
sucking my feet earthwards,
as I slip, rooted by the depths

of your grave, and come to realise:
death brings nothing to grasp
but the absolute ironies
of when and where.

In the dead of night an owl
hoots sorrow at my window
as if it were you.

Epiphany

I hear your heart beat strong and fast,
bringing more of you to my picture
of your twenty-week scan.
I wipe around your image on the fridge,
whisper good morning,
believing that you hear,
as you dwell, nonchalant,
thumb in mouth, appearing
to have all the time in the world.

Your shawl grows round by round
as I crochet each double and treble
in expectation, knowing it will be made
at the time you choose.

Quantum Poetics

What we might know intuitively
about the immeasurably
small

high energies of everything
we cannot see
nothingness exerting
her force.

Bosons transmit the weak
in the constant
creation - annihilation
of virtual particles
in the void.

The measurement problem:
in the act of observation
a created reality appears
until
you look for meaning.

Scape-Coat Poem

I weave a coat of words as remembrance
of the secrets lain hidden over the years.
This thread begins the stitch of your
deception, a wept tear on our wedding night,
for the young girl left alone as our babies grew,
and in turn, the silent, grieving
woman, turning to a shrew.
This pattern of circles, woven in grey and blue,
is for the times your drunken eyes stared
with hatred upon our children. This
yellow band is for the hand that beat me on
occasion, the black outline for the sorrow
you tried to feel. The sleeves, a patchwork
of green for the cold expanse of days
I suffered alone as your reputation grew.
The collar is red to match your rage when I
asked for love, the dots of pink depict
the chasm of neglect your children are left with.
This grows to the length of pain which I now
touch in remembrance of you, tentatively
at first, but soon this coat, mapped with our
battle scars, will remove the shameful chill
we suffered living with you.

A Glasgow Story

Encouraged by escalating disposable incomes,
the rich rushed west to Gilmore Hill and Kelvingrove
looking for a more fantoosh kind of culture.

Escaping from the reek of poverty and filth,
they left behind the Trongate and Cathedral,
in the hope of making something of themselves.

Today Glaswegians breathe fresher air,
where the notion of class has been abolished
by the possibility of appearing to have it all.

The modern way for accredited congregations,
now that bankers do God's work,
is the performance of ritual worship
at Silverburn, Braehead and Princes Square.

Communing in multi-culinary food halls,
hemmed in by designer-labelled bags
we drink our Fair Trade coffee and forget
we're not all Thatcher's bastards,
we're all Jock Tamson's bairns.

You don't know

that dolphins exist
that the sea is salty
what salty is.
You don't know
the scent of flowers
that love can hurt
what hurting is.
You don't know
that we can run
but birds can fly
what flying is.
You don't know
peace exists,
that without it
people die,
what dying is.
You don't know
atomic numbers
and what they signify,
you don't know
what it is
to signify
and why that might matter.

You don't know
the notion of sin
the immortal soul,

divine spirit,
the spark within,
and the conflict
they arouse.

You don't yet know
that to know
is a blessing
and a curse.

Oak-like

You can see I am the woman in the photograph
hugging that tree in Birnam wood,
with the Tay's white water gushing behind me.

What you cannot see through the lens, beyond
the black and white of bark and my flesh
is what it took to get me there,
how I am as I stand, arms
grasping the enormous trunk
of this ancient landmark
looking at you and smiling,
becoming oak-like.

Gravity

In the beginning
a cloud of dust particles
pulling in strange attraction:
matter and antimatter in equal measure,
creating the possibility of us.
A mere exchange
of photons, quarks and leptons
bringing our world together,
the influential glue of all that exists,
existed, or will come to exist.

Weak and powerful,
its hypothetical graviton transmitting the force,
slowing the tick of time,
vanishing into a place
beyond our reality,
seen without observation,
recognised by energy that appears
to disappear. Barely understood
yet we remain faithful
to having our feet on the ground.

In the beginning,
at the precise moment
before the nothingness stopped,
was there a will to creation,
a divine transcendence,

crazy enough to be truth?
The infinite mystery,
imminently present
beyond all
measure,
the unique
indivisible
absolute.

The Truth About Love

We speak with tongues, lips, hands,
using the power of body language
in the all-seeing darkness of intimacy.
I have barely heard you speak my name, happy
for our re-acquaintance with smell and touch.
Since you, I have discovered, it's not about
heart-beats-skipping, or feeling *complete*,
it isn't an equality of parts,
nor gazes, nor moons, nor stars,
though, I grant, that these things
have their place.

In our time we've navigated
questions of integrity, faithfulness,
tenacity, to reach our *coup de coeur*.

Notes on Love and Marriage

For Jenny and Barry, on your Wedding Day, 12-10-2014

Marriage is a mystery.
It is your own unique journey,
a personification
of love, and love's
complication.
It is intention, belief, passion
and truth, sometimes
a battleground with no winners.
It is a place of faith behind doors
for which only you
hold the key.

It is a recipe and you
are the ingredients,
it's made of what you make it.
It is oneness in the face
of division,
and acceptance when things go wrong.
It is a trier of patience and a giver
of joy, a bending path
across unmapped landscapes.

It is a hope; it's growing together
and being together against
the odds, a hill you climb
with magnificent views when you reach

the top. It's forgetting
the self and loving the other
when it's better to love than be right,
for if you have love, you have
everything.

Appearances

He advocates vitamins at lunchtime,
a life of celibacy,
ambiguous sexuality,
a game of tennis every day,
and wine from his vineyard in Portugal.

His sinister smooth skin and youthful looks
mingle with his mesmerising voice,
making women who should know better
abandon domesticity and wait for concert tickets in the
    rain.
I suspect this young one's place on earth
has been secured by beings from another galaxy,
beginning with his arrival one summer,
along with his Shadows,
on a double-decker London bus.

Moments

There is nothing between us that lasted
long enough to write home about.
We had fifty five minutes, give or take
a few hundred hours and ten thousand miles:
some meals together,
some afternoons of gossip and amorous talk,
    a touch,
walks along beaches, a party or two, formal engagements,
captured moments in hallways, under stairs, sharing
    cigarettes.
This secret, under mental lock and key,
causes questions to press in my mind,
questions about polarities, hemispheres and zones of time,
    not to mention
why there is nothing to write home about.

No Competition

The newsagent's sign on the kerb
confirms the news in black and white:
God will participate in the Perth Annual Run.
I stop to consider His racing plan,
omniscient, omnipotent, He's bound to win.
Not too busy with miracles,
or impeding cyclones,
to attempt this *fait accompli*.

Perhaps God craves the competition,
to prove He's still number one
among the elevation of egoists,
the fall of name-droppers,
transcendence of theologians,
scepticism of agnostics,
and one chap called Beelzebub,
who insists on being
competitor 666.

Commuter's Breakfast

To start,
the soft in-out of your breath
as you read *The Herald*
folded in four
across your firmly
muscled thighs.
Followed by
the way your hips hug
the centimetres of seat
claimed modestly on the 7.35
tossed with
the fertile suggestion
of your body's sway
with the tube as it shoots
through the fusion of subway lines.
Topped off
with long, brown curling lashes
flickering over a blushed
hint of stubble.
A side dish of parted lips
with your tongue playing
upon their form,
finished by our arrival
at your destination.

The Train to Heaven

'They call it Christianity. I call it Consciousness.'
Ralph Waldo Emerson

Stations stretch as a string of
pearls for her passing,
each with its tissue of facts.

The first stop is Charity, Good Works
is just round the corner, a guard announces
the entrepreneurs should get off here.
A few miles further, the city of Truth,
where priests drop in for light refreshments.
Not stopping at Humanity, she speeds
to the village of Hope where analysts
enlighten the resident population;
the people who live in Despair get off here.

And then to Peace, so small
it's not found on any map,
where officers of the United Nations
loiter in the limitless foothills.
The city of Faith has sister stations:
at Theology and Belief, old men and women
wield their tickets, but their tickets
have expired.

At the sub-station of Jesus, a choir
of a thousand gospel singers wave

their arms as we go by, as if showing
the way to Paradise.
God is the last stop before Heaven,
just after the crossroads at Satan's Loop.

Playing Away from Home

World Cup soccer playing on your TV
Bulgaria and Italy I believe.
You ask me the score and I tell you
while we play our own personal game
of participation, with you as the arbiter
of rule breaking. An own goal
in extra time, enhanced by adverts
for family holidays, echoes ironically
in this toy strewn room. The score
at full-time is ambiguous, you saved
a few penalties at my expense,
and in the communal shower afterwards,
I didn't know why it couldn't be
a win-win situation, then you
explained, those are the rules
of the game, especially when
playing away from home.

The Ten Commandments

Moses took notes,
hammering each letter into the stone
so that we might remember them
millions of decades later, but we have
ten fingers to prompt us, lest we forget.

Walking down from the mountain, Moses came
armed with his weighty tome of don'ts,
his tone imperative: Thou shalt
not do these ten things, otherwise
there will be trouble, he told the gathered
Sinai Massive staying away from the mountain and its edge,
for Moses had warned them, do that and you are a dead
    man
(for only he could see God you see).

For a start, we are no longer in the house of bondage,
we are free to worship just one God under heaven,
which He made. Any kind of art is out, statues, works in
    oil,
water-colours – these graven images are disallowed.
Television isn't listed, but it could be in an amended text,
hidden in St Catherine's vaults, along with that movie
by Cecile B. DeMille. Don't buy these works of art,
for god's sake, your love of them will make the big guy
jealous.

No worship in the National Portrait Gallery
or in your neighbour's living room, and stay away
from their life-partner too. Take out the garbage for your
  mum and dad
without swearing under your breath; no killing, no
  stealing
and no false witnessing, for that would be a lie.
Some lesser known commandments are obsolete,
we can't make our altars out of hewn stone,
and the big file of heresies is too numerous to list.

Periodic Madness

The urge to throw it all away
and wander with the travellers.
Monthly intuition calls us
to dance naked under stars,
disintegrate the glass ceiling,
dismantle the lexicon.

Adrift in circular time
thinking it will never end
forgetting that it always does,
requires resilience.

Taken by the insistent need
to stop and take stock
far from civilization
or simply to hang
upside down in the darkest corner
of a wardrobe
until we emerge brim full of energies
to nurture those who wonder about our time,
the enigma of mad women
and the other side they go to,
the side that needs more time.

Lighting up

Dunhill one milligram, gift-wrapped
box of gold and handy flip-top lid.
I reach inside repeatedly for those long,
white, smoking tubes with pale orange tips.
Lit in clandestine places, glowing remotely
in marked out spaces: after dinner, outside,
smoking zones with windowed walls,
in bed, in secret, while I make telephone
calls. Held resplendent between fingers
and raised to my waiting mouth, I
suck deeply upon their contained pleasure -
softly inhaling the essence of dragged
sensation; rushing to satisfy the soul,
slowly releasing the smoke from my mouth,
exhaling the cloud from my lips shaped
in an O, producing invisibility,
watching it go, and still seeking
the ultimate cigarette.

Pleasure Places

I have swept the inside of your teeth with my tongue,
felt the rough stubble of your chin and the hardness of
    your jaw
on my face. I have enclosed you with my body,
taken you in snow, on carpets and on the telephone.
We've rushed headlong on the beach before we were
    missed,
waited until after midnight when the house was asleep,
arriving from trains, in a car along quiet lanes,
in the master bedroom of the Wimpy Show Home,
cramped in the toilet of BA 012, where I have let you in.
I have urged you on when you have taken it slow,
shown you where you should go, helped you see
the secret places for our pleasure when you didn't know
how to be less urgent, lose your composure, give me
time, hear me breathe, know when I don't care where
I am, when I'm swimming outside myself using no stroke.

Choosing My Religion

I killed a fly and worried all morning.
Not being Buddhist, I worried in secret.
I walked to a shopping mall where an icon
of Christ hung on chains from the ceiling,
his pink lips moved but his words,
silence.

Standing stones are waiting for the solstice,
twenty-first-century rays gather
on obsolete rocks, their mystery
being the meaning of life,
an answer perhaps for lost
urban lambs, also
tarot, crystals and numerology,
chakras, star signs and homeopathy,
ecstasy, theosophy and colonic irrigation.

Candle

I am left in shadows to admire
this candle's mysterious body
burning slowly in its flaming wick,
serene within its wax forming
another shape. Its light is not the brief
flame of a struck match,
capturing moments of vision,
nor the cold white globe of wire and glass,
where nothing hides from its domain.

The candle's brief solidity
transfixes moths with its eloquent glow,
burns scented essence on altars
to virgins and brings solace to writers
in the night, the warm, lustrous
light of lovers in bath tubs,
among flowers on tables,
and through power-cuts.

Sundays Are Different Now

There is the ancient church
where we would offer praises
to a god we did not seek
to understand.

Rewarding ourselves with a feast
of eggs and bacon on our return home,
a starched white apron over mum's best suit,
bought every year to wear on Easter Sunday.
My brothers, my father and I savouring
a delicious end to the weekly four hour fast.

Sitting together in the same places,
communally gathering in the round
of a day set aside to meditate,
the strange possibility of being here.

Now there is no worship,
breakfast comes before lunch.
No fresh, crispy-white rolls
set among serviettes and tea-cups
saved for best.

Her white apron hangs redundant
as we eat solitary snacks from our laps,
having no time for the ceremonies of life.

The Automated Doors of the House of Poetry

In the magic eye above
the automated doors of poetry
I am never seen.
Its laser vision must be set
for greater heights,
because it misses me.
I leap sporadically at the sensor
alerting my presence to its beam,
but in my carnal intermittency,
it will not be deceived.
Whispered messages of 'I'm here' won't do,
no coded passwords like 'Open sesame'.
It takes more altitude to open the magic eye
of the hallowed halls of poetry,
where my precursors
keep spelling out my gloom.

Repossession

No matter how hard you try
it just can't be hurried
this day when you must decide
which treasures are expendable
by weighing up the memories
they hide, until just that moment
when nostalgia starts to fade, just
then, there it is, the object's silent plea
to remain as your possession.

No matter how hard you try
you can't ignore the van
outside, or its inappropriately
small size for all that you've
acquired, though you always
denied that you cared about stuff.
Yet here at this threshold,
you realise that valuing what you have
is how to avoid being a have-not.

Travellers

It must be very liberating
to rip the legs off your trousers
and call them shorts. Invigorating
to sit behind the wheel
of a converted ambulance
and call it home,
to search amongst the fallen
leaves of Autumn for mushrooms
and make them a meal,
to gather sticks and twigs
from the undergrowth
and cook by the fire's glow.
To rip the legs off your trousers
and call them shorts,
to make your address
from the sky's constellations.

Birkenau

The small toe on my right foot has blistered
walking the miles of your long, straight roads.
The soles of my favourite black suede boots
have come away from their uppers.
The heels are caked with the mud
of the swampy ground
between the ditches
Gypsies, Jews and Poles
were forced to dig –
pretence to stop
the inevitable floods
seeping through
the marshes,
through the slabs
of concrete,
through the straw
where they were
forced to lie,
six wide: the blister
on the small toe
of my right foot
will heal with time.

The Literary Life

I have found my place at Lumb Bank,
a wooden bench outside the communal dining room,
away from the poets. I light my cigarettes,
smoke in the chill air of critique,
watching Ted Hughes' abandoned garden hang
from the edge of a cliff it could fall over.
Ravens intimidate the silence
in dead trees on blue-black hills, blocking the sky,
trying to block the light of my mind.
I draw deeply on isolated addiction,
consider the destiny of my
overexposed and x-rayed words.
At this place, where rivals are star-crossed
bedfellows, across the black-rocked gulf,
I throw my doubt to the monument
made of all the cigarettes I am finished with.

Absolute Time

In memory of those lost on Air France Flight 447

You dropped at the will of air currents,
fell thousands of feet through clouds, stalling
while the automation disagreed,
as time took on another measure.

Long enough perhaps
to boil an egg,
run three and a half miles,
brush your teeth, down
a few shots of tequila,
update your status on Facebook.

Three and a half minutes
to approach the finite
nature of your life
approaching its end.
Are there cries of *not yet*?
Does a clarity come?
Do you seek comfort from strangers?

Making the last three and a half minutes
left to you matter, is a prospect
better considered before all that remains
is a plane seat, an orange buoy,
a barrel.

Isabella or the pot of basil

You came to me from your forest grave,
led me to see what my brothers had done,
and though I could no longer see your face,
faithful to love, I unearthed your head with my bare hands,
hid you in a shrine of basil, nourished you
with my tears. A kind of resurrection,
not life, but faith that nothing can be abolished
without trace, there is no end to the end.
Not pining, dying, I tend your garden head,
watch our herb of love flourish as I obsess
on a woman's fate to be pawned, bondaged
or exchanged, grieve my potential to create.

Bethlehem-Glasgow

Not born at the same time,
or even conceived together,
but choosing to be paired.
Dizygotic,
are we psychic
as twins might be?
Do we delight
in each other's triumphs,
feel what happens in the other's streets,
shriek at each other's losses?
We were founded
on Christian miracles,
cities of David and Mungo,
flourishing, and yet divided
through broken branches
of the same tree.
Our dear green place
reaches out to your little town,
breaking through the walls
you did not build.

Walking Monopoly

Start from Go by Conduit, between Regent Street and Bond
  Street
through Mayfair, Piccadilly Circus and Trafalgar Square
on Autumnal afternoons. The light is gloomed by unbroken
  cloud.
Indecisive winds and rain conspire to invert umbrellas,
billow raincoats and dislodge the hats of tourists wandering in
from Japan, Canada, Australia and the United States of
  America.
*Pick a Chance Card. Collect two hundred pounds. Move into your
  hotel.*
The National Gallery looks over the square and for twenty-five
  pence
you can have a cup of crumbs and pellets specially prepared
by the Greater London Tourist Board to feed
  the resident pigeons.
Go by Leicester Square, through the Strand and down
  Embankment
on the Thames, where workers sing from cranes to visitors
sailing in glass-topped boats that meander by Parliament and Big
  Ben.
Your dividend pays. A building loan matures. Get out of jail free.
Walk across Hungerford Bridge, step over the huddled
  children
slouched in corners of cold wrought iron:
their heads peep through the sopping blankets they are
  wrapped in,

begging in whispers with anonymous gazes
and self-effacing glances. Don't stop.
Keep pushing towards the Museum of The Moving Image
and Royal Festival Hall, where you can see 3D
plans to build an even better house for the Arts,
Community Chest: Go to Jail, Go Directly to Jail.

New Year's Day

Sitting on a Pacific Ocean cliff
at five on new year's morning
covered by a washed pink sky
where the moon lingers with the sun.
Fishermen wrestle their nets
while calling plans to each other,
their words fall away,
mingle with the sounds of birds
wakening in their colonies.
A new beginning here:
being in the world at dawn
as if all things can stay the same.

Printed in Great Britain
by Amazon